CW00850832

THE WNBA FINALS

BY CIARA O'NEAL

Apex is distributed by North Star Editions:
sales@northstareditions.com | 888-417-0195

Produced for Apex by Red Line Editorial.

Photographs ©: Rick Scuteri/AP Images, cover; Shutterstock Images, 1, 12–13, 16–17; Paul Beaty/AP Images, 4–5, 6–7, 9, 29; Frances Benjamin Johnston Photograph Collection/Library of Congress, 10–11; Buster Dean/Houston Chronicle/AP Images, 14–15; Chase Stevens/AP Images, 18–19; Susan Lesch/Wikimedia, 20; Ed Betz/AP Images, 22–23; Kamil Krzaczynski/AP Images, 25; Jim Mone/AP Images, 27

Library of Congress Control Number: 2022912150

ISBN
978-1-63738-296-7 (hardcover)
978-1-63738-332-2 (paperback)
978-1-63738-402-2 (ebook pdf)
978-1-63738-368-1 (hosted ebook)

Printed in the United States of America
Mankato, MN
012023

NOTE TO PARENTS AND EDUCATORS

Apex books are designed to build literacy skills in striving readers. Exciting, high-interest content attracts and holds readers' attention. The text is carefully leveled to allow students to achieve success quickly. Additional features, such as bolded glossary words for difficult terms, help build comprehension.

TABLE OF CONTENTS

CHAPTER 1

THE 2021 FINALS

One minute and 57 seconds remain on the clock. It's Game 4 of the 2021 Women's National Basketball Association (WNBA) Finals. The Chicago Sky trail the Phoenix Mercury by three points.

Phoenix's Brittney Griner takes a shot in Game 4 of the 2021 WNBA Finals.

Chicago's Courtney Vandersloot looks for an open teammate. She sees Candace Parker. Vandersloot passes the ball. Parker catches it and shoots a three-pointer. She scores!

COMING HOME

Candace Parker played 13 seasons with the Los Angeles Sparks. But she left the team in 2021. She joined her hometown team, the Chicago Sky.

Candace Parker (right) scored 58 points during the 2021 WNBA Finals.

The crowd roars. The game is tied 72–72, but not for long. The Sky outscore the Mercury, 80–74. Chicago wins!

FAST FACT

The Chicago Sky's win in 2021 was the team's first championship.

Courtney Vandersloot celebrates after the Chicago Sky win the 2021 Finals.

TOL 0 74 FOUL 05

CHAPTER 2

WNBA HiSTORY

Basketball is more than 100 years old. Women have played the sport for nearly as long. For years, no **professional** women's **leagues** existed.

High school girls play basketball in the 1890s.

The 1996 Olympics were in Atlanta, Georgia. Many basketball games took place in the Georgia Dome.

Then the 1996 Summer Olympics took place. The US women's team won the gold medal. More people wanted a women's league.

FAST FACT

The 1996 US women's team played Brazil in the gold medal game. The United States won 111–87.

The WNBA's first season happened in 1997. At first, eight teams **competed**. As of 2022, 12 teams battled for the **title**.

THE FIRST BASKET

Penny Toler scored the WNBA's first basket. She played for the Los Angeles Sparks. She made a jump shot against the New York Liberty.

The Houston Comets won the first four WNBA Finals.

CHAPTER 3

REACHING THE FINALS

W NBA teams play many games during the regular season. All teams play the same number of games. Only the best teams make the **playoffs**.

In 2022, each WNBA team played 36 games during the regular season.

A'ja Wilson and the Las Vegas Aces lost to the Mercury in the 2021 playoffs.

The playoffs are a **tournament**. Losing teams get knocked out. Winning teams move on to the next round. They play other teams that won.

FAST FACT

Going into 2022, Diana Taurasi had 1,455 playoff points. That was the most ever.

From 2011 to 2017, Maya Moore led the Minnesota Lynx to six of seven Finals.

The top two playoff teams face off in the Finals. They play a best-of-five series against each other. The winning team becomes the champion.

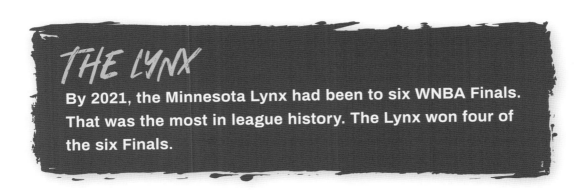

THE LYNX

By 2021, the Minnesota Lynx had been to six WNBA Finals. That was the most in league history. The Lynx won four of the six Finals.

CHAPTER 4

MOMENTS TO REMEMBER

The New York Liberty reached the 1999 WNBA Finals. They trailed at the end of Game 2. Then Teresa Weatherspoon sank a half-court shot. The Liberty won.

Teresa Weatherspoon (right) played in four
WNBA Finals.

Game 3 of the 2014 Finals was tied. Then Diana Taurasi drained an **off-balance** shot. Her team, the Phoenix Mercury, won.

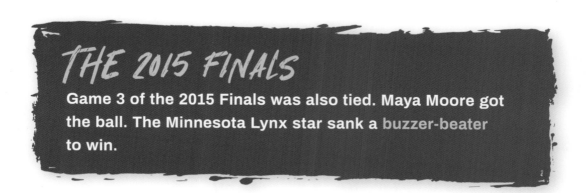

THE 2015 FINALS

Game 3 of the 2015 Finals was also tied. Maya Moore got the ball. The Minnesota Lynx star sank a buzzer-beater to win.

Diana Taurasi (right) shoots during the final seconds
of Game 3 of the 2014 Finals.

In 2016, the Lynx faced the Los Angeles Sparks in the Finals. They traded baskets at the end of Game 5. The Sparks took the lead with three seconds left. They held on to win the title.

FAST FACT

The Seattle Storm won their fourth title in 2020. They became the third WNBA team to win four.

The Sparks' Nneka Ogwumike (left) scores over Sylvia Fowles to win the 2016 Finals.

COMPREHENSION QUESTIONS

Write your answers on a separate piece of paper.

1. Write a sentence that explains the main idea of Chapter 2.

2. Would you rather watch the WNBA Finals or the Olympics? Why?

3. When did the Chicago Sky win their first championship?

    A. 1997

    B. 2014

    C. 2021

4. The Seattle Storm won their fourth championship in 2020. Before that, how many teams had won four championships?

    A. one

    B. two

    C. three

5. What does **drained** mean in this book?

Then Diana Taurasi drained an off-balance shot. Her team, the Phoenix Mercury, won.

    A. got rid of water

    B. made a basket

    C. got tired out

6. What does **battled** mean in this book?

At first, eight teams competed. As of 2022, 12 teams battled for the title.

    A. tried to beat one another

    B. tried to trick one another

    C. kicked and punched one another

Answer key on page 32.

GLOSSARY

buzzer-beater
A shot that goes in with no time left on the clock.

championship
The final game that decides the winner of a tournament.

competed
Tried to beat others in a game or event.

leagues
Groups of teams that play one another.

off-balance
Not on steady footing.

playoffs
A set of games played after the regular season to decide which team will be the champion.

professional
Having to do with people who get paid for what they do.

title
The top finish in a sports competition.

tournament
A competition that includes several teams.

TO LEARN MORE

BOOKS

Labrecque, Ellen. *WNBA Champions*. Mankato, MN: The
   Child's World, 2020.

Omoth, Tyler. *The WNBA Finals*. North Mankato, MN:
   Capstone Press, 2020.

Scheff, Matt. *NBA and WNBA Finals*. Minneapolis: Lerner
   Publications, 2021.

ONLINE RESOURCES

Visit **www.apexeditions.com** to find links and resources
related to this title.

ABOUT THE AUTHOR

Ciara O'Neal ate, breathed, and slept basketball growing up.
Nowadays, she's into writing books, wrangling her seven kids,
and teaching basketball tricks to her dog, Rocket.

INDEX

ANSWER KEY:
1. Answers will vary; 2. Answers will vary; 3. C; 4. B; 5. B; 6. A